"WITH PRIDE & DIGNITY"

The Life And Career Of Noble Fields

NOBLE FIELDS

ARCHWAY
PUBLISHING

Archway Publishing books may be ordered through booksellers or by contacting:

Archway Publishing
1663 Liberty Drive
Bloomington, IN 47403
www.archwaypublishing.com
844-669-3957

Interior Image Credit: Enrique G.

ISBN: 978-1-6657-1467-9 (sc)
ISBN: 978-1-6657-1468-6 (e)

Library of Congress Control Number: 2021922202

Print information available on the last page.

Archway Publishing rev. date: 05/24/2022

"WITH PRIDE & DIGNITY"

On Friday, January 23, 2004, I sat in Noble's office above her Real Estate School around noon observing the walls that portrays her life story. They held pictures of all the events that were important to her. From a small rural town in Oakwood, Texas emerged an energetic successful African American, a model of Madame C. J. Walker, an African American business entrepreneur who became the first black woman millionaire. As we began to talk, it was obvious that she had led a very interesting life, one that raised her self- esteem and made her very proud.

She was born to Jake and Mildred Lusk in 1935, who were hard workers and for the most part uneducated. Her father picked and chopped cotton seasonally and her mother did domestic day work in the homes of Caucasians. Noble considers that a point of her life that she does not care to reflect on a great deal. What she does remember however, she considers it a blessing in disguise although others may not see the connection.

She remembers her mother coming home from her father's funeral and telling her sister who was three years older than her, to start a fire so that she could prepare dinner This was a wood stove and to get the wood to start to burn it was necessary to pour kerosene on it, which she did but something unusual happened and in the next moment the house was in flames. She remembers her mother running to the bedroom and grabbing a white sheet to wave in the air to alert her father who was in the field about 3 or 4 miles down the road chopping cotton.

As the blaze got bigger and the black smoke became more visible, he looked up and saw her mother waving the sheet and came running. It was too late to save the house and it burned to the ground. They relocated to another small one room shack that was on the white owner's land where they resided as sharecroppers. This she remembers was the first turning point in her life. The tragedy was the blessing that became the instrument that would change her environment from what could have produced a negative disposition in her development. Shortly afterwards, (about one year) they migrated to Fresno, California. She remembers sitting in the Greyhound bus station and the ticket agent telling her father that he only had three seats on the last bus for that day and there were four of them. Her father told the agent he would hold her between his legs so that they all could get on the bus. As they left Texas, she remembers seeing a sign that spelled W-A-C-O, which was the last town in Texas that she remembers. In 1945 they arrived in Fresno, California another farm town only her

father wasn't doing the farming. When they first moved to Fresno her father's brother Josh, provided them with a place to live until they could rent a place of their own. He worked for Sun-Maid Raisin Company and was instrumental in getting her father a job there also. Noble was about ten years old when this move took place and believes that without this move, she would not have become the energetic highly motivated person that she became, The new environment provided her parents with a step upward in employment, housing and was the beginning of her education that provided her with the resiliency that would enable her to overcome adversities and persevere in her aspirations in turn raising her self-esteem.

They moved to 1148 Turland St. a diverse neighborhood that was comprised of Hispanic, Asian, Caucasian, and Black, and coming from a rural town in the south this provided her with a cultural awareness that she would not have experienced without the move. Their community was just outside of town but close enough for her and her sister to walk to the movie in China Town another first for her. She had never gone to a movie in Oakwood because there was no movie for African Americans to attend and if there had been it would not have been within walking distance from where they lived.

Noble's parents were not devout Christians who demanded that they attend church or any other religious activities. They lived directly across the street from a Catholic Church and she remembers the hospitality of the nuns each year providing them and other families with Thanksgiving

and Christmas dinners. Her parents always considered this to be a blessing but they never attended the church. For Noble, however, it was instrumental in providing her with what she now believes religion to be about. She does not believe that religion is about attending church every Sunday "toting a bible" to be seen and not speaking or helping people on Monday. The compassion of the nuns eventually led to her attending their services and later becoming a member. She recalls her mother attending a Baptist church and later a Pentecostal but she was never discouraged from attending the Catholic Church in order to attend services with her. She does not remember her father ever attending church except on rare occasions when he went with her to the Catholic Church after she became grown.

She attended Edison High School in Fresno and as a teenager she was interested in creative dancing and sports. She was on the girls' basketball team and a member of the gymnastics team. She showed enthusiasm about training and keeping in shape which her gymnast teacher recognized as a positive aspect of her development. With a big hearty laugh Noble recalled an incident in a gymnastics class when the teacher, recognizing her leadership ability allowed her to lead the class one day. She said she proudly went to the front of the class and very enthusiastically told them, "Okay class we're going to do twenty sit-ups," not realizing the difficulty of that task. As it became more strenuous, she told them, "Okay we'll settle for ten." The class had a big laugh and they were dismissed early

that day. Her solid self-esteem has never allowed her to be afraid to accept challenges and admit that there are times when she will not reach her goals. The important lesson is when trouble arises in our lives, the quicker we pick ourselves up after a fall, the more energy we must begin one more time. She would later learn that her enthusiasm for creativity and her physical ability would lead her to greater heights. It would provide her with the sense of competence that would inspire her to achieve and take pleasure and pride in her achievements.

Noble's peer group were girls from the neighborhood some of whom became pregnant and her mother would warn her that she should not hang around with those girls for fear of her falling into the same entrapment. The old saying of birds of a feather flock together was her mother's concern. She did not agree with this theory because she had her own set of values that provided her with resistance and strength to not be persuaded to do something that she felt was morally wrong. She attributes her mother's strict rule on this subject however, to the fact that she never had or wanted children. The other factor of course was the military which at that time if she had children she could not have remained in the army. This would have hindered her from reaching her goal of making a career in the armed forces.

Noble has always been an, extrovert and never feared not being good enough. She can take being teased without feeling devastated. She recalls being teased about her singing. At school she was singing the school song

to the tune of a popular song at that time and she said they called her in an assembly once to sing it. She guesses that it sounded pretty bad because some of her friends still tease her today about that song. Although she was an extrovert, she was only allowed to go on one date during her high school years and that was to her prom. Her date was a boy that was her next-door neighbor whom she liked but later was in and out of jail so she is glad that the relationship didn't become serious.

Noble graduated from Edison High School in 1953, with no definite plans for a particular career, but a yen to travel and visit Paris. She had often daydreamed about what it was like in other parts of the world. College was never a discussion with her by her parents or teachers, so she knew nothing about college. One day she saw some Caucasian women dressed in blue uniforms walking down the street. She thought they walked with pride and dignity as well as looking very chic in their uniform that was blue with gold buttons that glistened against the rays of the sun. This to her represented status and respectability. She called her mother to come take a look. She was told those ladies were in the WAVE. She decided then, "I want to wear a blue uniform." To pacify her, her mother bought her a four-piece blue suit the jacket, vest, skirt and pants that she could mix and match

in hope that this would take her mind off joining the navy. It was not a commonality that African American women joined the military mld they were not encouraged at all to join the navy. She recalls after she was inducted there was only five African American women stationed with her. Nothing however, could dissuade this self-motivated person and take her mind from the pride that those women had projected in those uniforms.

Her mother worked in a restaurant as a short order cook in down town Fresno. Noble would go down and help her in the kitchen by washing dishes. Although she had no idea in which direction life would take her, she knew that she hated this work and the only reason she did it was to help her mother who worked two jobs. When the owner of the restaurant heard her desire of joining the navy, he told her the recruiting office was down the street and that she should go and sign up to join. Knowing that her reasoning for wanting to join was because she didn't like washing dishes he told her, no matter where you go however, there's always going to be some dishes to wash. She said, "I know that, but I want to wear a blue uniform." To her, this represented honor, respect and discipline. She later learned that in the military she *would* wash dishes when she pulled KP, but that would be for a different reason. It would not be her career. She went to the recruiting office and signed up to take the test and failed. She

was told not to worry she could come back in thirty days and try again. Noble who is not afraid of failing refuses to accept failure. Therefore, she was not discouraged by this slight hindrance. Without determination she would not have gotten where she is today. She went back and failed again, but this time a woman from the WAC asked her what field she was trying to apply for. She had seen her there on the previous occasion. She said, "I don't know anything about a field, I just want to wear a blue uniform." She was told they had blue uniforms for certain occasions, why not apply to take their test because it was not as difficult the navy.

She did not know at the time that the test was used to deter African Americans from joining the navy. She took the test for the army and passed. This she considers her second turning point. She was inducted into the army on November 22, 1954, the same date, she later learned as she was being sworn into the army, Rosa Parks was being arrested for not giving up her seat on the city bus in Montgomery, Alabama to a white man. These two determined African American women would later take their place in the African American legacy of black women making a difference but on opposite platforms.

The military's slogan "You can be all you can be," would prove to be a true statement for Noble. Like a caterpillar that goes through a metamorphic change in becoming a butterfly that is set free to soar new heights so was Noble. Her first stop,

Fort McClellan Alabama, where she would complete her eight weeks of basic training. After completing basic training, she was given three preferences for her assigned station, New York, Europe or California. Her original desire to travel and see Paris was still in her mind and she felt that the military would be her best opportunity. Being the positive thinking person that she is she got part of her desire; she was stationed at Ft. Mason in San Francisco. As a child with, no role models and no one had talked to her about which academic road she should take, she entered the military with no skills and no idea of what training she desired. She was placed in an administrative unit that would train her to become a teletype operator where she worked in the hostess house. She learned that the key to success was education and flexibility. When she learned that the army had a talent contest every year she entered and won. The prize was traveling throughout the Far East entertaining. She was the only woman in the show which did not make the men too happy as she recalls. Because of her assertiveness this did not bother Noble and she did not feel threatened by this fact.

Being in the military protected her from the race riots and demonstrations that had begun although she knew of prejudice and realized that is was in the army as well only she had not encountered

any. One night she was at the NCO club with a mulatto friend named Ivory who would later become her husband and he didn't dance. A Caucasian man came over and asked him if he could dance with Noble. When they got on the dance floor the bartender came over and yelled no mixed couples. Ivory being the belligerent man that he was started a big commotion with the military. Three months later she received orders to go to Europe which she had been trying to do but to no avail. This was done to sweep the racial incident under the rug. She was stationed in Pirmasens, Germany and was able to tour all over Europe by entering the All Army Entertainment Show. She spent five years singing and dancing her way throughout Europe which was something she had always enjoyed doing, learning the language as she went another aspect of her education. This would mark the beginning of her road to success and begin her life as an entertainer. She actually entertained the thought that she might become a professional entertainer when she got out of the army. After being in Europe fifty-five days her sister died from sickle cell anemia, and she returned to the states to attend her funeral. This saddened Noble because her and her sister had been close while growing up. She recalls how her and her sister would play a trick on her mother. They would wait until about the time that their mother would be returning home from work and they would conspire to go and stand on the side of the road and pretend to be like orphans. When their mother would come home, she would say "What are y'all standing out here looking like little orphans

for?" and that would crack them up. Her mother and father separated also while she was stationed in Europe due to her mother's obsession with the house that she had purchased which made living conditions for him unbearable. *"Noble, she was always telling me where to sit, 'take your shoes off before you walk on the floor...'* and he finally got fed up and one day he picked up a hand full of mud and threw it in the middle of the floor and walked out. Noble being close to her father told him to live with his sister until she returned to the states. Upon her return she would make arrangements for him to live with her and become her dependent.

In 1962 she returned to San Francisco for duty at the Presidio base and because her father was going to live with her, out of respect for her father she married Ivory V. Fields. Common law partners were not as acceptable by parents for their children in those days by African Americans as they later became. Ivory was a civilian painter for the Air Force and Noble said it was a disastrous marriage. He was an alcoholic and his personality was difficult to deal with. She said because of her religious background as a Catholic she felt stuck. After being married for three months she received orders for Honolulu, HI another blessing in disguise because it gave her an opportunity to get away from her husband without divorcing him. In 1969, her last year in Hawaii she was asked to perform in a movie entitled "Kona Coast," starring Richard Boone and Vera Miles.

She performed and was paid $50.00, but after tax and other fees she received $35.00. She still keeps the receipt as a memoir. This would

also be the beginning of her real estate investments which would later become her biggest success story. She purchased her first 3 bedroom with 2 bathrooms home with her husband, which would be the first and last property that she purchased with anyone. When she was reassigned to San Francisco she sold this property for $36,000.00, which she had purchased for only $21,000.00, a gain of $15,000.00. This would be the beginning of her investing in real estate.

Upon her return to the Bay Area, she was assigned to the recruiting command station. Her duties were to visit local high schools and attempt to recruit them into the U. S. Army. Since she saw the army as a great advantage for those who were unable or had no desire to attend college this was an easy task for her. It's easy to promote something that you love and she loved the army. When asked how many she thinks she was responsible for recruiting, with a smile she guessed within the five years as a recruiter possibly a couple thousand. She believed in what she was doing. This also gave her another stepping stone in her education, as a recruiter she was required to spend time on television and radio promoting the army. The more qualified you are the better you are accepted. She decided to attend Columbia School of Broadcasting and the army paid her tuition of $800.00. She graduated with a third-class operators' license which entitled her to operate broadcasting equipment as well as become a media figure. This became instrumental in getting her an interview for a TV spot on channel 2 which she did not accept. She satisfied her ego

however, with her first live show on an FM radio station in Los Altos Hills where she played records, gave cooking tips and talked about the army.

From there she stepped into cable television and had two shows on cable 8 and cable 12 in Pacifica where she interviewed people from the community and featured free-form dancing to rock music as a body building technique. Channel 6 offered her a 30 minute show each week but she did not accept that offer She was doing all this while she was still in the army and she did not want to overload her plate. Noble squeezed television, radio, army and did modeling for a San Francisco designer and the time that she had left she devoted to her marriage.

Noble's marriage was an unconventional one of its time especially for African American women. For most of their marriage they resided in separate residences. He remained in Hawaii and they traveled to and from in between the states. She said that was the only way she could have remained married. She stayed married because she never intended to get married again. She believes that marriage is a sacrament and the vow is a contract that you should take seriously. If you vow to stay together for better or worse you should do that and not keep jumping in and out of marriage. These she realizes are just her own feelings about marriage. For this reason, she prefers to stay single and be a professional, this makes her happy. A disappointing marriage however, did not cause her to arm herself against intimacy with the fear of future hurt. She has a longtime companion of 30 years whom she says live at his place and she lives at

hers. They are compatible in the sense that he has never been married and neither of them wants to be.

After successfully completing 20 years in the military Sgt. Noble Fields retired in November of 1974 with a military ceremony on the Presidio parade grounds. Did this mean that she would join a retirement club and sit down and relax, or would she continue on to become successful in a second career. You can bet this energetic woman would not allow any grass to grow under her feet. This butterfly would soar on and taste the sweet nectar of life becoming one of the most successful women in the business world and helping others to become successful as well. Although she was very talented and enthusiastic, she says that was not enough. It took career planning, thoughtful schooling and a keen determination to beat the odds.

After retiring from the military Noble immediately became one of only two women to work for the National Alliance of Businessmen during that time, that partnership of business, labor and government that secures jobs and training for the disadvantaged, needy youth, Vietnam veterans and ex-offenders. She was selected as the Jobs for Veterans Manager over several applicants including a retired army major who told her that they were looking for a retired, black, disabled woman and she fit all those requirements. The selection process consisted of three personal interviews which apparently because of her training in mass communication and public speaking they were instrumental for her in securing the job. Her duties were to get pledges from employers which were offers of

employment, find veterans with the necessary qualifications to fill the positions and set up the interview. Since the interview is the impoliant link in the process Noble held seminars that included techniques in interviewing. She held seminars at the State Employment Development Department in SF, City College of SF and the Skill Center in the Hunters Point District where black women were made aware of the opportunities opening up for them in the business world. She said she was proud of her work in aiding the role of Black Women in business. She was awarded with an "Outstanding Service Award," for her work in developing a positive image for Black Women. She also taught an Upward Bound class at San Francisco State University. Noble said that out of an average of 100 veterans she would place about five because the problem was, they were not job ready. "Although school is important, experience is more valuable," she states. Noble pointed out that the image that employers had of the Vietnam Vet was that they were violent and unstable which they got from news articles. As a counselor she would teach them how to overcome these images. If they could show the good points of their army experience, they would get the job.

Black Veterans on the other hand according to this statuesque businesswoman, have a more difficult time securing a job. This woman who insists she's never been discriminated against, a bold statement considering she's black and a woman, says her eyes were opened in seeing the differences between the treatments of the black man as opposed to

the white man. Noble was well suited for her counseling position being trained in career counseling at Ft. Benjamin Hanison and working as both recruiter and instructor for recruiters before retiring.

To meet the challenges of life it is said one must achieve a learned major skill every seven years and have many strong accomplishments behind them. This is to continue from entrance to exit of life. Noble has mastered this concept. Her skills and accomplishments for the first half of her career are:

1. 20 years retired officer in the military
2. Talented singer and dancer, touring and performing in NCO clubs around the world
3. Performed for 10 years in Broadway clubs in New York, San Francisco and Hawaii
4. Promoted her own fashion shows
5. Hosted her own cable TV shows
6. Performed bit parts in major movie productions

For most of us it would take our entire life to become *so* versatile in our accomplishments, but for this energetic lady this is only the beginning. Noble is not your average person and definitely does not fit the stereotypical mold that society uses to label women and to add another label a "Black Woman." She is possessed with a drive that will not allow her to be content with standing still.

Although she is a disabled veteran and is connected with the Disabled American Veterans both local and national levels with a service-connected disability, she never allows that to slow her down. Just as she served her country with "Pride and Dignity" she is now a successful business woman with "Pride and Dignity."

Exchanging her sergeant stripes for a name tag that identifies her as a Realtor, Noble attributes the strict supervision and regimentation of the army for providing her with the morals and discipline that she needed in order to sustain her status in a business world that is usually dominated by the male gender. To keep herself motivated she would get up every morning and put on her uniform with the now different patches and badges which was a reminder of her purpose in life for that day. Noble's motivation to get into real estate was after she purchased and sold her first house in Hawaii and realized how lucrative the business could become.

As she states "Real Estate is a Noble Field." After spending time driving clients around looking at houses and them not buying, as she states "They were Lookie Loos," she realized that investing was a more lucrative business than wasting time with people who were just looking. So when she would take clients out if they didn't buy, she would make a deal through her broker using her commission for down payments.

Thus, she bought her first apartment building in Oakland and afterwards purchased other properties without her husband's knowledge. When they went through a divorce however, she bought her husband out

of the Oakland property and managed the building alone, thus giving her the experience she would later need later to handle other investments.

As she fore stated she learned the key to success is education which also raises one's self- esteem. After retiring from the military, she attended City College of SF and obtained an AA in marketing. She states she got just enough education to become dangerous. She bought propelty with gut feelings, not her head. If the bottom line was right, she would buy it. She said if she could get the down payment, she knew the rents would pay the notes. This was the way to allow real estate to work for you. She said ever since she began purchasing real estate, she has never had a foreclosure and all her mortgages have been current. Noble now owns 35 pieces of property in California and Hawaii. Noble was not satisfied to just obtain knowledge and keep it to herself. After retiring from the military, she had a desire to teach but she was not qualified to teach anything but military science. Being determined to rise to the challenge she began to prepare herself to become qualified to teach real estate as well and researched the possibility of starting her own "School of Learning." She learned while sitting in classes for her renewal real estate sales license that she could get approved to teach through DRE (Department of Real Estate) for completing 45 hours of continuing education. Upon completion of her 45 hours, she began marketing by placing a large billboard on the freeway. Confident that she could be a successful entrepreneur and take care of herself by earning her m:vn living and be happy doing it she opened

her first school and office in 1981, at 870 Market St., Suite 623, in San Francisco. Not willing that anyone should be go lacking in education because of inconvenience she later opened her second school in Oakland in a building that she already owned at 428 Oakland Ave, to service the community in the east bay. She recently purchased another building 4119 Mission St., in Daly City where she now has a third school. Noble has had students from Albuquerque, New Mexico, Reno, Nevada, and all around the states inquiring about her classes. At one time she was the only person authorized by the Department of Real Estate to give the lecture and the test in the area. Although it is necessary to receive the credentials for teaching, she believes the most successful instructor in real estate is one who has experience in buying and selling which she has. She has real estate holdings throughout California and Hawaii which is a total of 35 pieces of properties that qualifies her to teach from experience. She is authorized by the California Department of Real Estate to teach Residential Property Management, The New Ethics & Professional Code as Adopted by the Real Estate Commissioner's Regulation and Probate and Estate Taxes.

Although this woman who emanates such radiance from within has a skeleton in her closet that would throw someone with low self-esteem into a bout of depression. But this lady who celebrates life and accepts it as it comes told me a stoly that she only learned 60 years later. The father that she knew, she learns although, the only father that she knew is not

her biological father. After her mother and the father that she knew were dead, a woman contacted her who told her that she was her aunt. It seems that this was a lady whom her mother would go live with when she and her father were arguing. This aunt had two brothers and thus Noble was born. She was never told about this by her mother but she does remember her mother telling her if this lady ever contacted her, she was not to go see her or talk to her. Nine years ago, she went back to Texas to see this lady and discovered that she had two other half- sisters as well. She said she always felt the need to go back to her hometown but didn't know why because she did not know anyone there. Now she believes that this was her subconscious telling her that there was a missing part to her life. Now she feels complete.

Among her other numerous accomplishments Noble received a degree in law in 1991, from the Lincoln University in San Jose after being on academic probation three times. It took her 10 years to complete this degree, that's determination. An invitation she received that she calls her "Oscar" was in March of1998, when she was asked to speak at the Commonwealth Club of California. For a Black Woman who came from such a humble beginning to be given this honor was truly the highlight of her life which visible through her posture. This seemed to make her sit up straighter revealing through her body language the elevation of her self-esteem.

John's Bar & Grill | Friday, December 21, 2012
Miss Noble Fields jamming with friends.

John's Bar & Grill | Friday, December 21, 2012
Miss Noble Fields jamming with friends.

Black & White Ball | Saturday, June 2, 2012
Miss Noble Fields and friends.

Black & White Ball | Saturday, June 2, 2012
Miss Noble Fields and friends..

ARPB | Mayor Willy Brown | Miss Fields Friday, June 1, 2012
Mayor Willie Browns and school Director Miss Noble Fields.

Graduation Day at the Oakland Campus Site | Saturday, July 7, 2012
Miss Noble Fields presenting graduates their Certificates of Completion.

Miss Noble Fields | Sunday, September 16, 2012
Oral Lee Brown Foundation Luncheon and guests

Miss Noble Fields | Sunday, September 16, 2012
Oral Lee Brown Foundation Luncheon and guests

Miss Noble Fields | Sunday, September 16, 2012
Oral Lee Brown Foundation Luncheon and guests

Miss Noble Fields | Sunday, September 16, 2012
Oral Lee Brown Foundation Luncheon and guests

The Lovely Ladies Club| Monday, November 11, 2013
All you Lovely Ladies in the house, say cheeeese!!!

Miss Noble Fields & Jerry Lange Sunday, October 26, 2014
These ladies aren't showing any signs of slowing down yet!

License Renewals | Thursday, June 20, 2013
Continuing Education students just passed their tests!

Graduation Day | Monday, July 22, 2013
Graduates with their Certificates of Completion.

DC Campus | Saturday, February 6, 2016
Miss Noble Fields making preparations.

DC Campus | Saturday, February 6, 2016
Miss Noble Fields attending to her guest speakers.

Graduation Day | Saturday, February 6, 2016Miss Noble Fields & Certificates

Graduation Day | Saturday, February 6, 2016Miss Noble Fields & Graduates

Graduation Day | Saturday, February 6, 2016 Instructors Noble, Joe, & Graduates

Graduation Day | Saturday, February 6, 2016 Instructors Noble, Joe, & Graduates

Noble Fields School of Real Estate, LLC.
6121 Mission Street, Daly City, CA 94014
Cell: (415) 608-1388 Fax: (415) 594-0082
Noblefields.com *noblefields6@gmail.com*

Director Noble Fields and instructor Clarence Wise | Wednesday January 31, 2018

Miss Noble Fields living and enjoying life away form home
in Fresno, CA. | Saturday, September 14, 2019

Fresno, CA Tuesday, May 19, 2020
Miss Noble Fields' foxy look, love it!

Fresno, CA Friday, July 3, 2020
Miss Noble Fields' before shot.

Fresno, CA Friday, July 3, 2020
Miss Noble Fields' hair appointment.

Fresno, CA Friday, July 3, 2020
Miss Noble Fields' hair appointment.

Miss Noble Fields & Contra Costa Boys & Girls Club -Tuesday, May 19, 2020

Miss Noble Fields still going at the office. Tuesday, May 19, 2020

Miss Noble Fields on Hawaii 15 Day Cruise Tuesday, January 28, 2020

Miss Noble Fields on Hawaii 15 Day Cruise Tuesday, January 28, 2020

Miss Noble Fields on Hawaii 15 Day Cruise Wednesday, January 29, 2020

Miss Noble Fields on Hawaii 15 Day Cruise Wednesday, January 29, 2020

Miss Noble Fields on Hawaii 15 Day Cruise. Sunday, February 2, 2020

Miss Noble Fields on Hawaii 15 Day Cruise. Wednesday, February 5, 2020

Linda "Lou" on Hawaii 15 Day Cruise. Wednesday, February 5, 2020

Miss Noble Fields on Hawaii 15 Day Cruise. Wednesday, February 5, 2020

Printed in the United States
by Baker & Taylor Publisher Services